COMPLETELY
MISLEADING
HISTORY OF THE WORLD

Also in Beaver by Jim and Duncan Eldridge

How to Handle Grown-Ups
What Grown-Ups Say and What They Really Mean
Bogeys, Boils and Belly Buttons
More Ways to Handle Grown-Ups
BAD Boyes

And by Jim Eldridge
The Wobbly Jelly Joke Book

COMPLETELY MISLEADING
HISTORY OF THE WORLD

Jim and Duncan Eldridge

Illustrated by David Mostyn

BEAVER BOOKS

A Beaver Book
Published by Arrow Books Limited
62–65 Chandos Place, London WC2N 4NW

An imprint of Century Hutchinson Ltd

London Melbourne Sydney Auckland
Johannesburg and agencies throughout the world

First published 1988

Set in Century Schoolbook
by JH Graphics Ltd, Reading

Made and printed in Great Britain
by Anchor Brendon Ltd
Tiptree, Essex

ISBN 0 09 955730 4

Introduction

Allow me to introduce myself. My name is Peregrine Peabody and I am a Genius. There is nothing in this world (or any other world, for that matter) that I do not know. I know everything. Ask me any question about anything at all, and I can give you the right answer.

For some time I have been helping people by answering their questions. People I have never met before stop me in the street and say, 'Are you Peregrine Peabody?' When I say I am, they immediately ask me a question.

Because of this amazing talent of mine, lots of people have suggested to me that I ought to write a book containing my enormous amount of knowledge. This idea has always appealed to me. For one thing it would mean an end to my being stopped in the street all the time by people wanting me to answer their questions.

Among those people who urged me to put a book together are two writer friends of mine, Jim and Duncan Eldridge. They introduced me to their publishers, who were so impressed by my genius that they immediately begged me to write, not just one book, but a whole series of books. There is a simple reason for this: all the facts and knowledge contained in my brain are too many to be contained in just one book. And remember, much of this knowledge was only ever known to me before this day! That is why this book is so important.

So, here it is, the first in the series: *Peregrine Peabody's Complete History of the World* (although some idiot at the publishers has messed up the title on the cover and got it all wrong. Still, that's to be expected. After all, not everyone can be as perfect as me.)

So, open these pages and read them. And if you can't find the answer to your question here, then wait for the rest of the series. Or, stop me in the street and ask me. You will recognize me easily, I *look* like a genius.

Yours modestly but brilliantly,

Peregrine Peabody

Peregrine Peabody

The Beginning of the World

Once upon a time there was this enormous Bang! closely followed by a Pow! a Zap! and a Kerboom!! The next second this huge empty space, previously known as The Vast and Empty Universe, became known as The Vast and Almost Empty Universe, due to the fact that a planet was now floating in it.

The sun said to this planet, 'You're new around here, aren't you. Fancy going out somewhere?'

'I don't know,' said this planet. 'Call me Thursday or Friday.'

And so the new planet was called Thursday Or Friday. However, as calling it this made it feel a little week, it changed its name to Earth.

Fossils

The first living things on this new planet were actually dead. They were called fossils and were made of old fish-bones and lumps of rock with dents in them.

Fossils had a difficult time developing language, mainly because, as everything else on the planet was dead, there was no one to talk to. As a result, they didn't speak much to each other. This gave rise to the opinion that they were too High and Mighty to be bothered to talk to any other fossil, in which case they might just as well all die out — which they did.

The Ice Age

As everyone knows, the Ice Age was that time in early history when the ice-cream was invented. The very first mammal (known by scientists as Mr Soft Cone) had crawled out of the sea and straight into an ice-cream van, where it immediately invented ice-cream in six different flavours: vanilla, chocolate, pistachio, strawberry, cherry, and Tyrannosaurus Rex.

Unfortunately for Mr Soft Cone the only other creatures around at that time were the dinosaurs, and they proved to be allergic to ice-cream. As soon as they had licked it, they all died out, thus giving rise to one of history's Great Questions. What happened to the Dinosaurs? (answered here for the very first time).

Dinosaurs

Dinosaurs were all huge. That is, except for the small ones. They had names that no one could spell, names like ichthyosaurus, plesiosaurus, and the most dangerous name of all to spell, Tyrannosaurus Rex.

The length of their names was one of the reasons why they died out. (The other reason – their allergy to ice-cream – we have already discussed in the previous section.) As no one could spell their names, no one ever filled in forms about them, saying who they were. Because of this, as far as the authorities were concerned the dinosaurs Did Not Exist.

This meant that when they turned up to claim their unemployment benefit (there was not a lot of work about for dinosaurs, so most of them were unemployed) they were told by the clerks, 'I'm sorry, you do not exist.' This came as such a shock to them that they began to believe that they did not exist, and so they all died out. (The ones who were left, that is, after the Great Ice-cream Allergy of the Ice Age.)

The Bronze Age

The Bronze Age was when the world was at its sunniest, and everyone lay around getting tanned and bronzed. Very little is known about this time because the sun was so hot that nearly all the people lying around sunning and bronzing themselves got fried, and those that didn't get burnt to a cinder couldn't write. This has made it very difficult for historians to know what went on, which is why it is also known as The Dark Fried Bacon Age.

The Iron Age

The Iron Age was so called because it was the time when electric and steam irons were invented. This meant that at last Neanderthal Man could iron his clothes and look a little smarter when he went out hunting mammoths.

After a while, though, he noticed that however smart he looked when he first went out, after ten minutes of digging a mammoth trap the creases started to appear in his trousers again. It was at this point that he gave up hunting mammoths and started buying them instead. This is a practice that continues today, as can be seen whenever a store puts up a sign that says 'Mammoth Sale Now On'.

Interestingly, Neanderthal Man only started hunting mammoths by mistake after his next door neighbour, Palaeolithic Man, said to him one day, 'I'm going hunting a mammoth. Fancy coming?'

Neanderthal Man agreed because he thought they were going hunting a Mother Moth (Ma-Moth), and he thought he could handle that. When instead he saw this huge hairy thing with tusks galloping towards him, Neanderthal Man nearly died out on the spot.

Stonehenge

Stonehenge, found on the Salisbury Plain in England, is all that is left of a huge doorway leading to nowhere. ('Henge' was actually a misspelling of 'hinge'.) The stone hinge was one of two hinges used to attach the enormous stone door to the even more enormous stone doorway. By using the remaining hinge historians and archaeologists have managed to reconstruct a scale model of the doorway. This scale model is currently being exhibited in the Pretentious Prunes Museum in London.

By studying the reconstructed doorway historians have been able to make some guesses as to its purpose. The general opinion is that this doorway was a site of worship for ancient druids and was used as some kind of solar calendar. However other scholars contend that this theory is complete hogwash and the doorway was actually the start of a Wimpey building project which ran out of money after they built the first doorway on the estate.

Moses

Moses is reckoned to be one of the most misguided leaders in the history of Biblical times.

He is most remembered for leading his people to The Promised Land. For many years they followed him through desert after desert, until finally they settled in the only place in the Middle East that didn't have any oil under it.

The Ancient Greeks

The Ancient Greeks were really ancient. They were each about 180 years old and could hardly move.

They were always fighting battles against other people. Every time they discovered a new island they would launch a war against it. 'Look!' one of the Ancient Greeks would say, 'There's an island with just a goat on it. Let's declare war on it!'

Their most famous war was the Battle of Troy. This was all over a woman called Nellie, who was reckoned to be the most beautiful woman in the world. Over the years, however, she got less and less beautiful due to bashing her head against the side of a ship when it was first put to sea. This eventually gave her a face like an elephant. We know this from the famous line in the history books that tell us she had a 'face that launched a thousand ships'.

In this Battle of Troy the Ancient Greeks used a new weapon for the first time. It was called the wooden horse, and was a horse made entirely out of wood. However it couldn't gallop very fast, which is why they lost the battle, and also lost Nellie the Elephant.

Alexander the Great

Alexander the Great wasn't really very great at all. In fact at his school in Ancient Greece he was known as Alexander the Pretty Useless. This annoyed him a great deal, particularly because it meant that none of the other children would let him play with them. Another problem he had was that the rest of his class at school were all Big Heroes like Ulysses and Zeus and Ajax and Vim, who went out at lunch-time and did Heroic Deeds, while he sat in the school yard and lost at noughts and crosses to the school cat. They would come back in the afternoon and he'd say, 'Hello. Had a good lunch-break?' and they'd say things like, 'Pretty ordinary. Went out and found a Golden Fleece and killed a Gorgon. What about you?' And Alexander would say, 'Oh, I played conkers.' Then all the Heroes would laugh at him and go and play football, and they wouldn't even let him be linesman.

Alexander got so fed up with this that he came up with a plan. He went around Ancient Greece chalking on walls 'Alexander is Great'. At first people just laughed and sneered, but after a while they began to believe it, and pretty soon the Heroes started to invite him to play games with them after all. By this time it was the cricket season, so he looked a bit of an idiot when he ran out on the pitch in his football strip. Still, they let him play, because everyone said he was Great. Unfortunately for him, he was out first ball, proving that you can't win them all.

The Seven Wonders of the World

The Seven Wonders of the World were famous things that were around in Biblical times (well, at least in that part of Ancient History). They are VERY FAMOUS things and everybody knows all about them and what they were. In fact they are Incredibly Unbelievably Famous and Very Well Known and Quite Amazing. The Seven Wonders of the World were:

1. The Hanging Gardens of Babylon. This was a fantastic garden in Babylon (a small town just outside Melbourne in Australia) in Ancient Times that hung from the window box of a very tall house. It had everything in it: fuschias, blue flowers, red flowers, yellow flowers, leaves, and all the other sorts of things you find in hanging gardens.

2–7: The other six Wonders of the World.

The Great Wall of China

There are three Great Walls in history. The Great Wall of China is the first of them. It is so called because it is truly magnificent. It is amazing. To describe the Great Wall of China accurately is almost impossible – it's tall and high and strong and thick and very long. Well, it's pretty big, really. Some people say the Great Wall of China is the only man-made object visible from Space. I cannot say for sure whether or not this statement is true as I myself have never had the opportunity to see the Great Wall of China from Space.

The Wall is thought to have been part of a Youth Training Scheme for unemployed teenagers in ancient times. These youths were set to work building a wall which served no apparent purpose other than to keep them out of the ancient dole queue.

Because of its name, many people think it was built in China, but they are wrong. It was in fact built in Stoke-on-Trent, England. It was called the Great Wall of China because it was built from loads of smashed-up porcelain.

Confucius

Confucius was an old Chinese sage. (Sage is also a herb, as in 'sage and onions'.) This caused Confucius a lot of trouble, because when people asked him who he was and he answered, 'I am Confucius, the sage,' they used to pop him in the pot of whatever it was they were cooking. This did his clothes no good at all, and eventually they shrank so much that they almost strangled him. It was at this point that he stopped calling himself a sage.

Confucius became famous for coming out with clever sayings (e.g. 'Confucius he say, he who laughs last has taken longest to work out the joke.') He was always coming out with phrases like these. He would wake up and immediately say something like, 'Confucius he say, man who gets up early has happier life than man hit on nose with bamboo banjo.' Then he would go down to the street, accost some passing stranger and give him a line of similar wisdom. Eventually the people in the town became so desperate to avoid being stopped by Confucius and given a Good Thought that they employed a watchman to warn them of Confucius's approach.

In order not to hurt the old philosopher's feelings they told him nothing about this. The plan was that when the watchman (Dim Wang) saw Confucius approaching, he would run around flapping his arms and quacking like a duck. This would be the signal for everyone to run and hide until Confucius had gone.

This form of activity (running around madly flapping your arms like a demented duck) was named after Confucius, and was known as 'confusion'.

Poor old Confucius soon noticed that there was no one around for him to give his Wise Sayings to, so he set up a Chinese Christmas Cracker Company and put his Wise Sayings on bits of paper in the crackers instead – a tradition which still exists today.

The Pyramids of Egypt

What very few people know about the Pyramids of Egypt is that they are actually upside down. The original design had them pointed at the bottom and with a large square flat top. They were intended as a coffee table and chairs for a race of giants who inhabited that part of the Earth at the time, and who had ordered a set of enormous furniture from Pharaoh Ramese Spencer XXIV, a well known Epyptian interior decorator.

Unfortunately the foreman that Ramese put in charge of the work, Ug the Idiot, had the plans upside down as he gave orders to the slaves for the construction of the furniture. So when the giants came to test out their new suite by sitting on it, they all injured themselves quite severely. Ramese Spencer XXIV had to go into hiding while the giants roamed around Egypt looking for him to demand their money back.

Hannibal and the Elephants

One of the Great Moments in animal history was Hannibal crossing the Alps with a herd of elephants. Why he did this is not really known – the most usual suggestion made by historians is that Hannibal was an elephant trainer in a circus. He was doing a moonlight flit across the Alps to avoid the Finance Company repossessing his elephants for not paying their food bill.

Whatever the reason, it gave rise to this notable conversation between two Ancient Onlookers, Vice and Versa, as they watched the procession of elephants, led by Hannibal, lumbering across the mountain range.

VICE: *'Good Heavens!'*

VERSA: 'What?'

VICE: *'There's a flock of elephants over there!'*

VERSA: 'Herd.'

VICE: *'Heard of what?'*

VERSA: 'Herd of elephants.'

VICE: *'Of course I've heard of elephants.'*

VERSA: 'No, no, an elephant *herd.*'

VICE: *'So what, I've got nothing to hide.'*

VERSA: 'Hide from what?'

VICE: *'Hide from an elephant.'*

VERSA: 'Of course you get hide from an elephant!'

VICE: *'I know, and there's a flock of them over there.'*

Ancient Rome

Ancient Rome was a terrible place to live in if you were a Christian or a slave. Christians were forced to play in the weekly football game against the Lions, and the result was usually Lions: 10, Christians: Nil.

Slaves had no rights at all and were usually flogged to death if their master or mistress had a headache.

However, if you were a Roman then things were pretty good. You were allowed to wear a toga, which was a long white sheet. This meant you could dress up as a ghost and knock on your friends' doors and frighten them when they opened up, by shouting 'Boo!'

Rome was ruled by the Seizers, so called because they seized most of the good things in the city – jewellery and gold, etc. The most famous Seizer was Julius Seizer, who was the most famous man in the world of his time, and used to speak in Latin. As everyone else spoke Greek this made life a little difficult for him – as no one could understand what he was talking about. In this way he started a tradition for Heads of Government that continues unto this day.

The Seizers were all named after the months of the year (July – Julius Seizer; August – Augustus Seizer; June – June Seizer, and so on). This meant that after the twelfth Emperor, Decemberus Seizer, died they had run out of names, so the whole Roman Empire collapsed.

Hadrian's Wall

As I said before, there are three Great Walls in history. This is the second one.

Hadrian's Wall became a Great Wall by accident. Hadrian had a little house on the border of England and Scotland on the west coast, and he decided to build a wall at one end of his garden to stop his neighbour's dogs running in and out. He drew up plans for his wall and sent them in to the local Council, who approved them, and passed them on to a local builder to carry out the work. The Council Clerk who sent them to a builder rolled the plans up with the drawings on the outside, as was the normal practice with plans. The builder, however, who was new to this bureaucratic way of doing things, had never seen plans rolled up before, and he assumed that this meant that the wall just kept going on and on and on as he rolled the plans over.

He kept building the wall until he reached the east coast, where he fell into the sea.

Attila the Hun and Genghis Khan

Attila and Genghis were two of the original vandals and hooligans. They used to walk about all over Ancient Europe and Asia, wearing big boots, kicking people and frightening them. Between them they originated all the chants that are nowadays heard at football matches. One example of this is, 'Ere we go, Ere we go, Ere we go!' Although they claimed the credit for this, they did not in fact make it up. They stole it from the last words of Attila's tame earwig as it fell over a cliff, which were: 'Earwig—O!'

During their Vandalism tour of the Whole Ancient World, Attila and Genghis came up against many other local vandals and hooligans, who used to bash Attila and Genghis over the head with as many blunt instruments as they could lay their hands on. In the early days this caused Attila and Genghis quite a few headaches, so they had their brains removed. After that, they could be hit over the head without feeling any pain whatsoever. They could also use their heads for knocking against walls and demolishing them, and as a place to keep their woolly hats. This 'having-your-brain-removed' is a tradition that still exists amongst modern vandals and hooligans.

The Saxon Invasion of Britain

It was in about 400-and-something that Ancient Britain was invaded by the Saxons, the Angles and the Jutes. Not much is known about life after this invasion, which is why it was known as The Dark Ages, mainly because the Saxons etc didn't bring any light bulbs with them when they invaded.

The *Saxons* were so called because they invented the saxophone, which was the name they gave to their language. The peculiar thing about their language was that it was spoken through a long, bent metal tube with holes in it.

When they invaded Britain the Saxons named the parts they conquered after themselves, e.g. Essex was named after the East Saxophones; Sussex was named after the South Saxophones; and Middlesex was named after Fred Middle, who'd come over with the Saxon invasion by mistake because he thought it was a day trip to Dover.

The other invaders who accompanied the Saxons were the *Angles* and the *Jutes*. The Angles were so called because they were all bent at 90 degrees due to a National Plague of Back Ache. At least, that is what it was thought at first, until it was discovered that the reason the Angles all walked around bent over was because their braces were all caught in their shoelaces.

The Jutes were a very small invading army. In fact there were only two of them, Martha and John Jute, and they both fell over the cliffs on the Isle of Wight while walking around looking for people to conquer.

The Anglo-Saxon Chronicle

The Anglo-Saxon Chronicle was the first national daily newspaper ever published anywhere in the entire world. As printing had not yet been invented, each copy had to be written out by hand by Saxon monks, and all the pictures in it had to be drawn and then coloured in. This meant that the paper's circulation was very low. In fact its circulation was only one copy a day, and it wasn't long before the paper was losing money.

In a desperate attempt to boost sales they brought in new features: namely Page Three pin-ups and Bingo. As all Angles and Saxons and Jutes (and the few surviving Ancient Britons) were all in love with horses, the Page Three pin-up was of a horse. This proved very

popular for the first two issues, but after this readers complained that all the pin-ups looked the same.

Bingo was not a success at all. As no one could recognize numbers, everyone in the country thought they had won every time there was a game, and they used to turn up in their thousands at the newspaper's office (a monastery) to demand the prize (usually a picture of a horse). This always led to a riot, and usually resulted in the Editor being beheaded. (Incidentally this is how the job of 'editor' got its name, because they used to be beheaded by having their *ed* (Saxon spelling of 'head') *it* (Saxon spelling of 'hit'). *Editor* thus means 'a person who has their head hit'.)

All in all, therefore, the Anglo-Saxon Chronicle was not a success and died out after a thousand years or so.

The Vikings

The Vikings were a warlike tribe who had horns on their helmets, so that they could beep them to let people know they were coming. This was a good idea as far as other people were concerned, because the Vikings' major occupation was going out and looting and pillaging. They would set the alarm for about half-past seven, and when it went off their leader would say, 'Right lads, time to go off and pillage and loot!'

Then they would jump in their boats and head off for the nearest country (which often happened to be Ancient Britain) to loot and pillage.

They had a tradition of burning their boats whenever they arrived at the country due to be looted and pillaged. At first this was thought to be so that they had to stand and fight, giving rise to the legend that Vikings never surrendered. In fact it was because the Vikings thought it was the only way to stop their boats as they didn't have brakes on them. They used to get the fire going ten metres from the shore so that by the time they reached the beach the boat would have burnt away. It was about a hundred years before they discovered that they didn't need to do this because boats didn't need brakes anyway. By then it was too late – they had run out of wood and couldn't make any more boats. This meant they had to give up looting and pillaging. Instead, they just walked around looking miserable and beeping the horns on their helmets at each other.

William the Conqueror and the Invasion of England

The time was 1066 (also known as 6 minutes past 11) when the Normans invaded England at Hastings. They were known as the Normans because they were all called Norman, except for their leader, who was called William I.

His name had originally been William Indiana de la Snodgrass, but when his birth certificate was being made out, they only managed to write 'William I', and then they ran out of paper. They told William later that this stood for William First. This was why in any battle he was always in the front of a charge, so that the final result would always be: William First, Normans Second.

The English were led by Harold 'One-Eye' Goodwin, a fish salesman from London. He happened to be on holiday with his firm's annual outing to the seaside at Hastings when the Normans arrived.

The Crusades

The Crusades was the work carried out by the first ever international First Aid organization, the Crusaders. People who joined it used to wear a coat with a big red cross on it, and then they would be sent overseas to International Wars to look after people injured in the war.

Although it was a good idea in theory, in practice the two sides taking part in the war mistook the red crosses for targets. To solve this the Crusaders changed the name of their organization to the Red Cross. This had no effect whatsoever, so, being exceedingly irritated, the Red Cross changed their name back to The Crusaders, and killed everybody.

Magna Carta

Many people ask, 'Where did King John sign Magna Carta?' The answer is, on the dotted line at the bottom.

Magna Carta is Latin for 'Big Cart', and it was a law to make things fairer for everyone in England by giving them all a big cart each. This created terrible problems as people could only pull a big cart if they had a big horse. So there was another uprising and another piece of paper for King John to sign, called 'Magna Horsa'. It stipulated that everyone in England must be given a big horse.

As there were not enough big horses to go round, the Government had to resort to drastic measures. They imported a load of little horses and tried to pass them off as big horses by:

1. Standing the little horses on bricks. This became known as *highering a horse,* later altered to *hiring a horse* or *horse for hire.*
2. Blowing them up with a bicycle pump. Unfortunately a national newspaper got hold of this story and published it with the headline: 'Horse Blown Up. Terrorists Suspected.' So this method was dropped.

Pretty soon afterwards the whole idea of Magna Horsa was also dropped.

Some people wanted Magna Carta dropped, too, but because it was based on A Principle it was kept, and so the whole of England became swamped in huge carts that were too big to be pulled around and never moved. This was the first ever official traffic jam.

Leonardo da Vinci

Leonardo da Vinci was a Genius. He was a painter and a sculptor. He also invented the first flying machine, the first computer, the first tee-shirt, and the Leaning Tower of Pisa. He was *also* the first person to discover anatomy and work out how people worked. In his spare time he *also* used to do a bit of plumbing, building and decorating. He *also* did window cleaning, and he *also* had a milk round in Venice. As Venice is built on water and all its streets are canals, it made it difficult for him to walk from his milk cart to people's doorsteps to leave his bottles of milk.

After nearly drowning a few times, he switched on his Genius brain and invented a milk cart that could travel on water. He called it The Milk Float. He then replaced his usual horse with a horse that used to be a water-polo pony, and thus became the most famous milkman in Italian history.

The Peasants' Revolt

It was King Englebert IV who was responsible for this. His Chancellor came to him one day and said, 'Sire, I think the peasants are revolting.'

'Revolting?' said Englebert. 'If you ask me they're downright disgusting.'

This annoyed the peasants so much that they rose up against him and decided to go to London and kill him. Luckily for Englebert the buses were on strike that day so the Revolution had to be postponed until the following Tuesday.

The following Tuesday it rained, so the Revolution was called off until it stopped. By the time the weather cleared up and the buses had started running again, it was Thursday, and by then the peasants had forgotten what the row was about, so they all went home.

The Plague

The Plague was a dreadful disease which swept England, killing thousands and thousands of people. It was also known as The Black Death because just before they died they turned completely green. (At this time the colour 'green' had not yet been given its name, and any colour that people were unsure of they called 'black'. Hence the Black Knight was actually a bright yellow, the Black Mountains were purple, and Black Magic was really a funny sort of orange colour.)

The cause of The Plague remains a mystery. One theory is that it was brought to England by rats who lived on ships. Another theory is that it was caused by the population eating too much rhubarb, which caused large numbers of people to swell up and burst. A third theory is that it was a germ that came from Outer Space and infected the whole country. *Another* theory is that all these theories are just guesswork, because all the doctors died in The Plague, so there was no one left who knew for certain what had caused it.

The Hundred Years War

Few people know that the so-called 'Hundred Years War' actually lasted for only ten years. An error was made when details of the war were being recorded, and a clerk accidentally added another nought on. This other nought made it The Hundred Years War.

The war was started by King Edward III, a pompous twit who for some crackpot reason felt that he had a right to the throne of France. Edward had a son who was also called Edward (another of these Royal coincidences which causes great confusion in the history books and is one of the reasons why it is so hard to remember which king was which).

Edward's son Edward was nicknamed The Black Prince, although nobody really knows why. There are many suggestions as to the theories most often advanced are that he never washed and therefore ended up looking black and grimy; or that he was an anarchist who dressed all in black.

The rest of the Hundred Years War (or Ten Years War) is really not very interesting. All you need to know is that the English never had a hope in hell of getting the French throne, and they didn't.

Joan of Arc

It was originally thought that Joan of Arc was in some way connected with Noah and his Ark, but this theory has recently been proved wrong, since Noah was around thousands of years before Joan, so there is no way that these two people could have been connected, except they both had something to do with Arks (or Arcs).

Now that we have managed to eliminate the Noah-Joan connection we can get on with finding out the truth about Joan of Arc. It has been conclusively proved that Joan had nothing to do with Arks of any kind, so no one knows why she was called Joan of Arc (or Ark). Joan is thought to have played some part in defeating the English in the Hundred (Ten) Years War, although recent historians have said this was nothing to do with her at all — it was her brother John who fought for the French in the Hundred (Ten) Years War.

As a matter of fact I'm not really sure what Joan is doing in this book at all since it appears she had nothing to do with Noah, Arcs (or Arks), or the Hundred (Ten) Years War.

Henry IV

Henry IV was actually a commoner whose real name was Henry Ivy, but due to confusion at his birth and a clerical error he ended up as King of England, Henry IV (or Henry the Fourth).

Few people know the truth about Henry Ivy. The hapless man tried to tell people who he really was, saying over and over again, 'I'm Ivy, I'm Ivy.' But people at the royal court took no notice – they assumed they had yet another Mad King on their hands. Henry's situation wasn't improved when he was found climbing up the outside walls of his castle one day. Although he explained that he had got locked out and was trying to climb in through a window, the royal doctors assumed that the King had finally gone round the bend in his belief that he was a wall-climbing plant, and he was removed from the throne.

Marco Polo

Marco Polo was, as everyone knows, the man who came to fame after inventing the 'Polo mint'. When Marco was asked what made his mint so special he simply said, 'This is a Holy mint.'

Although it is a well known fact that Marco invented the famous mint, few people know that he also invented a game which was named after him – Polo. The game of Polo consists of people galloping around on horses and knocking Marco's famous mint around with a whacking great mallet. This rather pointless and idiotic caper was thought up by Marco Polo after a night of heavy drinking with some friends. Apparently he and his friends had a competition to see who could come up with the stupidest idea for a game, and Marco won.

Christopher Columbus and the Discovery of America

Christopher Columbus discovered America by accident. When he set sail from Spain in Fourteen Hundred and Something he was actually intending to discover Italy. This was because he had seen it on a map and noticed that it was shaped like a boot which is kicking an island called Sicily. He had recently had one of his boots stolen by a Sicilian, so, thinking that any boot that could kick a Sicilian was a good one to own, he set off in search of it.

Unfortunately for him he took a wrong turning as he left the port, and ended up instead in America, still wearing only one boot. He realized it was America because of the skyscrapers that had been built all over the place by the original Americans, the Red Indians. As modern building methods had not yet reached America, the Indians were still using the wigwam technique. Some of these wigwams were twenty storeys high, an incredible achievement for the time. One problem was that the lifts kept breaking down, and the Indians who lived on the top floors were fed up with climbing up and down the stairs all the time.

When Columbus and his crew arrived they looked just like the men in the adverts who come to fix lifts. Because of this the Indians welcomed them with open arms and allowed them to take over the country. Four hundred years later the lifts still do not work properly.

Caxton and printing

Caxton was the person who first discovered printing. He did this after his father gave him a Home Printing Outfit one Christmas, with all the little letters made out of rubber. Unfortunately for him he didn't realize that he had to put the words in back to front when he was making up the words for printing. This meant that his very first publication, a book of poems by William Shakespeare, read as follows:

> bmal elttil a dah yraM
> dup emos dah osla ehS
> mut reh ni pu dexim tog owt ehT
> .doog os leef t'ndid ehs dnA

Because of this mistake, this book was not a big seller.

Caxton didn't have much luck with his second one, either, because as he was putting it together he dropped his little rubber letters 'a' and 'o', and his cat ate them before he could pick them up. As a result his second book, a collection of jokes by Genghis Khan, read like this:

Witer, hve yu gt frg's legs?
N, sir, I lways wlk like this.

After the failure of this book to sell more than one copy (and that was bought by his mum), Caxton decided to give up printing as a bad job and left it for someone else with a bigger printing set to discover it a bit later on in history.

Henry VIII had six wives who were all called Jane, except for two of them, who were called Doris and Wilma. He got rid of most of his wives the same way he got rid of most of the people around him, by beheading them. This became known as 'cutting people dead' or 'cutting someone off without a penny', a practice still carried on today, though without the same sharpness.

Queen Elizabeth the First
New Zealander

Many people think that Queen Elizabeth the First of England was the daughter of Henry VIII. They are wrong.

Elizabeth was actually the daughter of a Maori chief from Wellington, New Zealand. (Although at the time it was not called Wellington, because Wellington hadn't yet been out there to name a town after himself.) (In further fact, the country was still so far from being discovered by anybody except the Maoris that it was called Old Zealand.) After her father died Elizabeth claimed the chieftainship of her tribe in Old Zealand, but her claim was contested by another Maori called Maui. To settle the dispute it was decided that the two should set off in a canoe, and the one who brought back the most treasure after four weeks of canoeing should be the new chief.

Elizabeth set off at once, canoeing at high speed. Unfortunately for her the villainous Maui had stolen her compass, which meant that she didn't have any real idea of where she was going, so instead of going west, where a legendary golden land was said to lie, she went north, and a fortnight later she paddled up the English Channel and landed on the beach at Brighton.

Coincidentally Henry VIII, the King of England at that time, had just died, and his daughter Princess Mary Queen of Scots, who also called herself Lizzie, was in Paris leading the English troops against the French. The

King's court had sent word to Princess Mary, urging her to come home immediately and take the throne of England in her father's place, and they were all anxiously standing on the beach at Brighton looking out over the sea, when Elizabeth landed in her canoe.

MARY?

NO! ELIZABETH!

By the time Princess Mary Queen of Scots arrived, the beach at Brighton was deserted, and when she claimed to be the true Queen of England everybody just laughed at her and she was locked up in the Tower of London.

Elizabeth decided to stay (mainly because her canoe had got a hole in it as she dragged it up the beach, so she couldn't go back to New Zealand anyway), and she ruled England and everywhere else in the world for the next ninety-seven years.

As for Maui, his canoe sank three days out of New Zealand and he was eaten by sharks.

The courtiers were a bit annoyed at this canoe suddenly appearing on the beach when they were expecting a Royal Visit, so they sent a passing fisherman to ask the canoeist who she was. The fisherman ambled over to Elizabeth, who was still dragging her canoe up the beach, and said, 'Hello. Who are you?'

'I am Elizabeth,' said Elizabeth. 'I am from New Zealand.'

'Good Heavens!' said the fisherman. 'You're the first person from New Zealand who's ever come to Brighton.'

'Who is she?' demanded the royal courtiers.

'Elizabeth,' called the fisherman, 'The first—'

But before he could add '—person from New Zealand who's ever come to Brighton,' the royal courtiers fell on their faces on the sand in homage, welcomed her as their Queen, apologized for not recognizing her instantly, and took her back with them to London for the coronation.

Sir Walter Raleigh

Sir Walter Raleigh was famous for (a) inventing the bicycle; and (b) bringing back two amazing discoveries with him from America: (1) tobacco, and (2) the potato.

Although the bicycle nearly failed because he forgot to invent a saddle for it, his major tragedy was in getting tobacco and the potato the wrong way round. That this is so can be seen in a letter he wrote to Queen Elizabeth I shortly after his two momentous discoveries. (Three, if you count him jumping on his newly invented bicycle and

ANOTHER ROAST TOBACCO?

NO THANKS — I'M TRYING TO GIVE THEM UP!

discovering that it hadn't got a saddle.) This is his letter:

Dear Illustriouſ Queen Majeſty Elizabeth, Ruler of Half the World and all of the Known Univerſe.

Today I hath discovered a most wonderful new plant with a most unusual property. To deal with this plant you take the leaves from it, dry and shred them, then set light to them and inhale the fumes. I am going to call this new plant 'the potato'.

I hath also discovered another new plant which I am calling 'tobacco'. This is an edible plant, much like the turnip, and it can be eaten boiled, fried, mashed or roasted. I am sure it will meet with great success. I hath already opened a shop on the East Coast, a Fried Tobacco and Fish Shop, which I am convinced will do well.

As to the potato, there I hath devised a most ingenious way of making my fortune from this plant. I hath rolled the shredded leaves of potato inside thin tubes of parchment, which thin sticks I intend to sell by the rod, pole and perch, with a Government Health Warning on the side of each packet. These thin sticks I intend to call 'the chip', and I shall be opening another shop to be called a 'Chip Shop'.

It was as a result of this confusion that Sir Walter Raleigh was recalled to England by Elizabeth I and beheaded.

Sir Francis Drake

Sir Francis Drake is famous for being the first person ever to set sail with the aim of travelling completely round the world in a boat. He did this to prove to everyone that the world was round and not flat, as most people believed. Unfortunately for him, no sooner had he passed Spain than his boat fell over the edge, and that was the last anyone saw of him.

William Shakespeare

William Shakespeare is the most famous playwright in the entire history of playwrighting. However, some literary critics and historians believe that his plays were actually written by Sir Francis Bacon, another writer who lived at the same time. The evidence they give for this is as follows:

Shakespeare's most famous play is called 'HAM*let*' about a *Danish* prince. The critics and historians say these were clues put in by the writer to let us know that the play was written by someone called Bacon. Another theory is that this play was originally called *Omelette*, then *Ham Omlet*, before being finally called *Hamlet*, and these are clues to let us know that the real writer was actually Sir Francis Egg.

Among Shakespeare's (or Bacon's, or Egg's) other Most Famous Plays are: *Romeo and Noddy*, *King Leer* (also known as *I'll never Smile Again*), *The Taming of the Hamster*, *All's Well That Turns Out Alright*, *O Fellow!* and *Macbeth Meets Godzilla*.

The Gunpowder Plot

The Gunpowder Plot was an attempt by a man called Guy Fawkes to blow up the Houses of Parliament. His reason for doing this was because he had stood eleven times as a parliamentary candidate and each time he had failed to get elected. Unable to bear the thought of printing thousands of leaflets for the twelfth time, and for the twelfth time making speeches on street corners where people threw rotten vegetables at him, he decided that if *he* couldn't be an MP, no one would.

Fortunately for the Government, but unfortunately for Guy Fawkes, the plot was discovered when a constable noticed a horse and cart unloading hundreds of barrels of gunpowder outside Parliament. This aroused his suspicions, and he ordered the driver of the horse and cart to stop unloading the barrels (which had 'GUNPOWDER' written on them). The constable then opened one of the barrels and looked in it to see if it really was gunpowder. As it was dark inside the barrel, the constable lit a match to see better. The explosion that resulted started the Great Fire of London.

Oliver Cromwell and the Civil War

The Civil War in England was between the Roundheads and the Cavaliers. The Cavaliers were those people who were on the King's side, and the Roundheads all had round heads.

This was very unfortunate for those people with round heads who supported the King, it meant that they had to go and have plastic surgery to have the shape of their heads altered.

It was called a Civil War because the attitude of each side to the other was very civil and polite. A typical exchange would go like this:

CAVALIER: *'Excuse me, but I believe you are a roundhead.'*

ROUNDHEAD: 'By heavens, that is a very intelligent observation! Yes, I am! Are you, by any chance, a Cavalier?'

CAVALIER: *'Yes, it so happens I am.'*

ROUNDHEAD: 'Well I never! I would like to say what a pleasure it is to meet you.'

CAVALIER: *'Likewise, I assure you. It indeed delights me to have the pleasure of your company.'*

Then they would each get out a weapon and kill each other.

Isaac Newton and Gravity

One day Isaac Newton was sitting under an apple tree when – Wallop! – an apple fell on his head.

'Good heavens!' he said. 'This is gravity!'

Actually he was wrong, it was a Golden Delicious, but this is the moment when gravity was discovered. Until that time everyone had floated a few centimetres above the ground. The discovery of gravity made a major difference to World History, because at first people couldn't move at all. Because of this new gravity they were actually stuck in one spot. This caused the collapse of all the major travel firms of the time, because no one could move to go anywhere. It also stopped all wars because no army could move in any direction.

All this was changed, though, in Seventeen Hundred and Something, thanks to the invention of the roller skate by Lady Janet Wheels. Her invention meant that people could move again. All the travel firms recovered, and wars could start again.

The Pilgrim Fathers

It was one day in Sixteen Hundred and Something that the *Mayflower* set sail from Plymouth, packed with Puritans off to start a new life in America. The interesting thing is that the Puritans had no idea where they were really going – they thought they were off on a trip round the Isle of Wight. What happened was this:

The Puritans were very pure people who spent all their time on their knees praying, and walking around the streets looking for bad people to preach at, telling them to See the Error of their Ways. As most of the other people around at the time who weren't Puritans were bad people, this meant the Puritans spent an awful lot of time on their knees beseeching people to repent. This was all right in their own living rooms, but when they did it in public the pavements became clogged up. Soon the whole of Society was on the point of falling apart because no one could move for Puritans kneeling down praying everywhere. Things got so bad that the Union of Muggers, Thieves, Pickpockets and Yobboes sent their representative to see the King.

'Sire,' said the representative of the UMPTY, 'we beg for your help. Business is terrible. Our victims can't find their way down dark alleys because of all these Puritans kneeling all over the place. As a result of this we can't earn any money.'

The King (a member of UMPTY himself

before he won the crown in a newspaper Bingo Contest) saw the problem, and called his Court Advisers to him for help. The answer they came up with was an advertisement in the newspaper:

'BARGAIN FOR ALL PURITANS
A Trip Round the Isle of Wight
Be at Plymouth docks at half past ten.'

Thus it was that when the *Mayflower* landed in America some six months after the Puritans had first set sail, they all believed they were on the Isle of Wight, and it wasn't until a hundred years had passed that they realized they were wrong.

The American War of Independence

It was in the 1700s, after they realized that what they were on wasn't the Isle of Wight but America, that these newly named 'Americans' got decidedly fed up with the way they had been treated over the whole Isle of Wight affair and decided to ask for their money back. This was refused as the travel company that had organized the trip had by then gone out of business.

It was then that a really clever American Senator, Seamus O'van Grubelschnikker, came up with a brilliant idea.

'If they won't give us our money back the proper way, then we shall get it back from them by other means,' he said.

'How?' asked Congress.

'Simple. We shall declare war on Britain, claiming that it is a War of Independence. Then, very simply, we lose, and as compensation for us losing the British will have to pay us millions of dollars.'

'Why?' asked some of the Congressmen.

'Don't ask me why,' said O'van Grubelschnikker, 'but that's the way it works. The winning side always has to occupy the losing side and pour millions of dollars into the economy.'

It was generally agreed that this was a brilliant idea, and that losing a war with Britain looked a fairly safe option. To do the whole thing in the nicest way possible they announced that there would be a Tea Party at Boston when all the necessary paperwork organizing this War of Independence could be signed, but as no one from the British Government turned up the whole thing fell a bit flat.

'What do we do now, clever clogs?' Congress asked O'van Grubelschnikker.

'No problem,' said the Senator. 'We go ahead with the plan anyway. We'll attack something British on July 3rd then we'll surrender on July 4th.'

So on 3 July a party of two Americans and a dog attacked an empty toilet on loan from a British Sewage Company just outside Boston. On 4 July the British surrendered and claimed compensation of millions of dollars from the newly Independent American Government. This is why, in the whole American celebratory calendar, there is no O'van Grubelschnikker Day.

George Washington

George Washington was the first President of the United States of America. The Americans were so proud of him that they named their capital city after him – New York. (His full name was George New York Washington.)

George Washington invented everything in America (e.g. lightning, false teeth, the rubber banjo), but he told everyone that it was Benjamin Franklin. He did this not because he was modest but in case anything went wrong with one of his inventions and he got sued because of it.

Washington is most famous because he Never Ever Told A Lie, a tradition which has been strenuously rejected by every American President ever since. This 'Not Telling A Lie' occurred most famously when he was a small boy and he chopped down his father's favourite cherry tree. His father was very angry and said to him, 'George, who has chopped down my favourite cherry tree?' Quick as a flash George replied, 'Father, I cannot tell a lie, I did it.' His father was so impressed by this truthfulness that he said, 'George, because you told me the truth, I forgive you. And here is a dollar for your honesty.'

A little later George accidentally chopped down his family's outside toilet. Again his father came to him and said, 'George, who has chopped down our outside toilet?' And George answered, 'Father, I cannot tell a lie, I did it.'

This time his father belted George around the head.

George was astonished (as well as hurt) and complained bitterly, 'But father, when you asked me who had chopped down the cherry tree and I told you that I did it, you praised me for my honesty and gave me a dollar.'

'That was different,' said his father. 'I wasn't sitting in the cherry tree when you did it.'

The French Revolution

The French Revolution was different from other countries' revolutions because it happened in France. Apart from that one fact, it was very similar: the poor rose up and killed the rich, took over, and were then in turn governed cruelly and harshly by some of the people who used to be poor but who then became rich. However most of the French poor didn't realize this was what was going to happen, and they went along with the Revolution and continued chucking aristocrats into carts and taking them off to be guillotined.

The French Revolution actually started in the buffet of a Paris Railway Station. There was a big fight going on for the jam sandwiches, and the Queen, Marie Antoinette, managed to grab the last one. A hungry train driver protested that he and his guard had seen that jam sandwich first. Quick as a flash Marie Antoinette cracked back, 'Have some cake instead!'

Unfortunately this did not go down too well with the train driver, as cake always brought on his indigestion, so he threw a jam doughnut at the Queen. The next second the whole buffet was in uproar and the French Revolution had begun.

The most famous figures of the French Revolution were Danton, Sombody Else and The Scarlet Pimple. The Scarlet Pimple was actually an Englishman who used to rush in just as the crowd were about to guillotine a French aristocrat, and save him from death. The Scarlet Pimple would then take all the grateful aristocrat's wealth, and then return him to the crowd and the guillotine. This way he became a Hero to everyone, as well as getting very rich.

The discovery of Australia

In the eighteenth century Britain was suffering from an excess of convicts. The prisons were so full that the Government started putting convicts wherever there was a spare bit of space. Soon ordinary citizens couldn't move for people chained up together. In desperation the Prime Minister, Lord Thing, called for Captain Cook, a brother of Captain Bird's-Eye, and said to him, 'We're running out of space. If we don't do something soon the whole country will sink under the weight of all these convicts. Go off and discover Australia, and then we can send them there.'

So Captain Cook went off and returned a couple of years later, having discovered Australia. By the time he returned, however, Britain had been completely overrun by the convicts, and they were now in charge. So the convicts, not wishing to leave, chained up the Government and all the law-abiding citizens and sent them to Australia instead.

Beethoven

Beethoven was the first ever deaf piano player and composer. Not only was he deaf, he also didn't have any arms or legs, and it was rumoured that his head was actually only kept in place by a bolt through his neck.

Despite these handicaps he was a brilliant pianist, and amongst his many compositions were *Grieg's Largo* (possibly the best tune in the world), *Tchaikovsky's 1812 Overture, Handel's Water Music* (which featured a tap on a pipe), and *Be-Bop-A-Lula*.

He was also a well known player of brass wind instruments. He could play the trombone with one nostril, and he was very good on the cornet, whether it was strawberry, vanilla, or chocolate.

Napoleon

Napoleon was a famous French General who became the leader of France. He is usually pictured standing with big boots on, watching a battle with his hand inside his coat. The reason he stood like this was because he couldn't find a belt big enough to fit him, so he kept his hand inside his coat to hold his trousers up.

At the end of his military career, Napoleon was sent into exile to New Zealand, where he started a spaghetti farm, growing spaghetti on trees that were five metres high, and macaroni on little bushes. As a sideline he also planted potatoes and knives in the same ground so that they would come up as chips.

Wellington and the boot

Most people know that the Duke of Wellington invented a large rubber boot, which was named after him. What most people don't know is *why* he invented it. This is the reason.

In his early days, before he became a duke, when he was just plain ordinary Fred Wellington, he lived in a bed-sitter in a large house. Every night Wellington used to come in late, at about half-past eleven. He would sit on his bed, take his big heavy boots off, and drop them on the floor with two enormous THUDs. This used to annoy the man who lived in the bed-sitter below, a workman called Joss Biggerstaff, because it meant that every night he was woken up by one Thud, then another Thud.

Finally, after two weeks of this, Joss could take no more. He grabbed hold of Wellington and said, 'Listen. I am fed up with being woken up every night by you coming in and dropping your big heavy boots on the floor. If it happens again I'll come upstairs and personally stuff both those boots down your throat.'

As Joss was a very large man, Wellington promised that it would not happen again. However, that night at half-past eleven, Wellington lurched in, straight from the pub, having completely forgotten his promise to Joss about the boots. He staggered up the stairs to his bed-sitter, sat down on his bed, took off his left boot and dropped it on the floor with an enormous THUD!

Suddenly the memory of Joss's threat popped into Wellington's head, and the dreadful realization of what might be about to happen to him if he woke Joss up. So, still wearing his right boot, Wellington climbed into bed and went to sleep.

About an hour later he was woken up by a loud banging on his door. Nervously he called out: 'Yes?'

'For pity's sake,' roared the voice of Joss Biggerstaff from the other side of the door, 'drop the other boot!'

Because of this incident Wellington went out the next day and invented a large rubber boot, which he could drop on the floor without waking people up.

The Invention of the Railway Train

The railway train was invented by George Louis Stevenson in between writing *Jekyll and Hyde* and *Noddy Invents The Railway Train*. He stole the idea from another Scot, James Watt. James Watt was in his kitchen one day when he noticed that there was a lot of steam coming from the spout of his kettle.

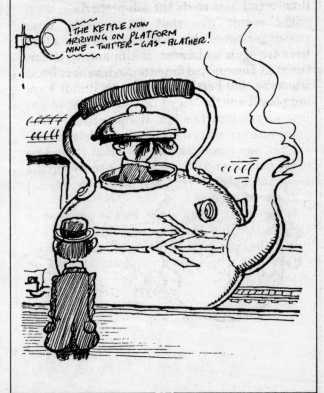

THE KETTLE NOW ARRIVING ON PLATFORM NINE – TWITTER – GAS – BLATHER!

'Wow!' he said. 'If I put wheels on that kettle all that steam should make it move along.'

So he put wheels on it, but all that happened was that the hot water ran out through the holes where the axles were. He went round to his friend, George Louis Stevenson, to borrow a kettle to make a cup of tea, and told him what had happened. George pretended to be sympathetic, gave him a cup of hot water, then rushed off to make a giant kettle with waterproof axles and so do the job properly.

The result was that four months later passengers were able to buy tickets on the first ever Glasgow to London steam kettle. Unfortunately George had forgotten to invent railway tracks for his kettle to run on, so it didn't get very far. Thus the very first railway kettle was late arriving in London. It was actually four years late arriving, because it took that long for the railway line to be built. By that time most of the people who were waiting to travel on the train had walked it, so the first journey was not a financial success.

James Watt, meanwhile, was so annoyed at Geroge stealing his idea that he went off to invent the light bulb. He did this because he was determined to get his name immortalized on something.

The American Civil War started like this: Abraham Lincoln, who was the American President at the time, was attending a play written by Henry Wilkes Booth, the founder of the Salvation Army. The play was in full swing when Lincoln suddenly had a Great Thought, and he stood up and declaimed loudly, 'You can fool some of the people all of the time, you can fool all of the people some of the time, but sure as eggs is eggs I still don't know where belly button fluff comes from.'

The actor on stage at the time, Herman McCready, was so upset at having his big speech interrupted that he pulled out a gun and shot Lincoln dead. This act caused national disagreement: most of the people in the South thought the actor was quite right to shoot Lincoln because they felt that as a gentleman, Lincoln should at least have waited until the interval to say his piece. In the North, however, where the population consisted mostly of theatre critics who had all hated the play, they condemned the man who had shot Lincoln. ('After having seen this play I am of the opinion that Mr McCready shot the wrong man, he should have shot the playwright.' – *New York Times Stage Review and Marrow Growers' Gazette, 1865.*)

The result was a Civil War, in which the North marched South and the South marched North, thus leading to geographical confusion.

The final result was:

The North: 485,000 dead; 3,647,986 wounded.
The South: 598,000 dead; 4,197,437 wounded.
The Chicago Bears: 68.

The American Wild West

The American Wild West was not a healthy place to be. This was because the place was full of people with names like Wally the Kid, One-Eye Jake, Peg Leg Peregrine, etc etc, who were all hardened gun-slingers and went around shooting people and spitting tobacco on their boots. As if that wasn't bad enough, the Wild West could only be reached after a three-thousand-mile trek in a covered wagon, which was attacked and burnt to the wheels every twenty kilometres or so by marauding Indians with names like Sitting Bull, Standing Horse, and Kneeling Raccoon. In fact the whole thing was nearly as dangerous as travelling in the rush hour in the present day.

Amongst the most famous figures of the old Wild West were:

Billy the Kid: so called because he was only three and a half years old.

Wiry Twerp: Marshall of Tombstone City. He called himself The Fastest Draw In The West, but he wasn't really. In fact he couldn't draw at all, he could only colour in pictures with crayons, although he could do that quite fast.

Hopalong Pussyfoot: a one-legged gunfighter.

Jesse and Frank James: a pair of buskers who played banjo and spoons.

Jim Bowie: inventor of the knife of the same name. Starved to death waiting for someone to invent a fork to go with it.

Davy Crockett: invented a hat made of fur with a raccoon's tail hanging down from it. Unfortunately for him, he thought the tail hung down the front and he spent most of his life walking into trees as a result. He died after falling over a cliff. After this tragic accident the Mark II Davy Crockett hat had the tail at the back.

General Custer

General Custer was an Indian fighter in the last days of the American Wild West. He used to walk round looking for Indians to pick fights with. Generally he was a clever fighter, because he would go into a bar and say 'I feel like a fight. Any Indians here?'

If his challenge was accepted by an Indian of under two metres high and with no muscles, then he would go Biff! Bash! and claim another victory.

If, however, his challenge was taken up by someone like Geronimo, or Crazy Horse, or any Indian who could obviously pound him into dust, then Custer would say, 'Not you. I'm challenging Indians from India. Anyone here from Delhi or Bombay?'

When no one came forward he would go, 'Aw, shucks,' and then slope off, claiming that they were too scared to come out and fight.

Unfortunately for him he began to believe his own stories of always being victorious, which led to him challenging any Indian in America to a fight at the Little Big Horn stadium on Thursday 12 March 1897, and offering a prize of four dollars to any Indian who could beat him. On the day a hundred thousand turned up to have a go at winning the prize, half of them Indians and the other half cowboys and saloon girls disguised as Indians.

When Custer woke up on the morning of 12 March and realized what was in store for him, he thought and acted quickly. He put on a feather head-dress, painted his face with war paint, and went along to the Little Big Horn stadium at the appointed time. He waited five minutes, then shouted out to the assembled crowd, 'Looks like Custer ain't coming! Guess he must be dead! Well I ain't waiting any longer!'

With that he walked out of the stadium, and everyone followed him.

The scramble for Africa

In the nineteenth century Africa was full of explorers from Britain, Belgium, Holland and other such places, all walking around claiming bits of it for their countries. This had all started because word had gone around the European capitals that an explorer called Dr Heineken was walking across Africa claiming it in the name of Ruritania. The major European countries therefore sent out their explorers to go ahead of him and claim the parts that Heineken hadn't yet reached.

In fact, as often happens, the story had got confused in the telling, so that by the time it reached Europe everyone had got hold of the wrong end of the stick. What actually happened was this:

A certain Dr Livingstone (not Heineken) was an ex-explorer who now lived in the African jungle. In another part of the jungle, over two hundred kilometres away, lived a family of apes. Now the smallest ape of the family was a tragic figure because he had been born without any knees, and this meant that he couldn't walk. His family were very sad and used to carry him around, but the littlest ape was very independent and insisted on being left to take care of himself. One day an explorer called Stanley came upon them, and the apes told him the tragic story of the littlest ape.

'There is an answer,' said Stanley. 'In the jungle, about two hundred kilometres away, there is a doctor called Dr Livingstone. He is the best doctor that ever lived. He has performed operations on other animals in the jungle to help them walk by giving them artificial knees. I am sure he can help your littlest ape.'

The apes were delighted at this, but their hopes fell when Stanley said, 'There is only one problem. Dr Livingstone insists on a token payment from his patients towards the cost of building a hospital for sick animals in the jungle. Have you got any money?'

Sadly the apes shook their heads, they had absolutely nothing. Their forlorn faces touched Stanley's heart, and he took out his purse and gave them a penny.

'Here,' he said. 'It is only one penny, but Dr Livingstone will perform the operation for this.'

And with that Stanley went on his way. The ape family were overjoyed and wanted to rush off straight away and carry the littlest ape to Dr Livingstone, but the littlest ape was firm.

'No,' he said. 'I want to be independent. Give me the penny and I shall go and see Dr Livingstone on my own.'

So the ape family gave the littlest ape the penny, and off he went, crawling and dragging himself through the jungle. Through swamps he went, through thick forests, and across the lands where lions hunted. His journey took him six months, but at last he dragged himself into the clearing in the jungle where Dr Livingstone was supervising the construction of his hospital for sick animals. Wearily, his fur torn from his hazardous journey, the littlest ape dragged himself up to where Dr Livingstone was standing. Livingstone looked down at the littlest ape in surprise, and said, 'Can I help you?'

'Yes,' croaked the littlest ape. 'Have you got two ape-knees for a penny?'

(Note from Peregrine Peabody for young readers: in those days Britain had a different money system with a big large penny, which was worth two half-pennies [pronounced 'ape-knees'] .)

Art: the Impressionists and the Post-Impressionists

The Impressionists were so called because they used to do impressions of famous people in history while they painted their pictures.

The leading Impressionists were:

Vincent Van Gogh: Vincent Van Gogh was a Dutch artist. He wanted to paint so very much that he cut off his ear. Unfortunately it didn't work very well as the paint kept running off it, and he had to go back to using brushes instead.

Toulouse Lautrec: He was a very short French painter – so short that he slept in a matchbox. He used his height as means of getting out of lending people money. When Van Gogh or one of the other painters said to him, 'Toulouse, can you lend me a couple of francs?' he would say, 'I'm sorry but I'm short today.' He was always a very busy painter, which earned him the nickname No Time Toulouse (No Time To Lose).

After the Impressionists came the Post-Impressionists, who all worked for the Post Office.

Queen Victoria and Albert Hall

Queen Victoria had the longest reign in British history. This meant either that the weather was at its worst when she was queen, or that she rode a horse with a longer neck than anyone else's. Whichever it was, she was not amused. In fact she spent most of her life not being amused, as can be seen by her expression on the postage stamps of the time. All this changed, however, when the man she fell in love with entered her life – she married him and they lived happily ever after. This man was called Albert Hall, a music hall comedian who she met at a Royal Command Performance. He made the Queen laugh with jokes like:

'What's got four legs and flies?'
'I don't know, what has got four legs and flies?'
'Two pairs of trousers!'

Unfortunately all the rest of the Royal Family looked down on Albert, so he was not allowed inside Buckingham Palace. This meant that their marriage consisted of him standing in the Mall shouting jokes up at Victoria's window through the railings of Buckingham Palace, and being regularly arrested for behaviour likely to cause a breach of the peace.

The Boer War

The Boer War was half fought in the Dutch language, which is why there is confusion about how to spell the title of the war.

One reason it was called this was because it was run by really boring generals.

Another reason was because these generals armed their soldiers with pigs and boars, which they used to throw at each other and hit each other over the head with. This throwing of pigs and boars never achieved much as they were so heavy it was all the soldiers could do to pick them up, let alone throw them.

The Boer War came to an end when the RSPCA stepped in and had it banned, claiming it was cruel to pigs and boars who were getting a pretty raw deal out of being chucked about all over the place.

Victorian Writers

All writers in Queen Victoria's day wrote enormous thick books that weighed at least five kilos each. This was part of a Keep Fit programme that Queen Victoria wanted to try out on the nation so that all the people who lived in Britain would be fit. People would go into a shop, buy a book, and then develop huge muscles walking around carrying it.

Amongst the top two writers of the Victorian age were:

Charles Dickens: He wrote so many books that his publisher couldn't publish them all. This meant that he was forced to publish many of his books under other names. These included: *The Falling Knickers* by Lucy Lastic; *Who Broke That Window?* by Eva Brick; *Spring Is Here* by Teresa Green; and *How To Play Steel Drums* by Lydia Dustbin.

Jane Austen: Some people say she was not a Victorian writer, since she died two years before Queen Victoria was born. But they are wrong. Jane Austen was famous, not only because of the books she wrote, but because she started the Austen car factory at British Leyland some years before Henry Ford actually invented the motor car. Because of this some people thought she was far-sighted and forward looking and a visionary, but most people thought she was an idiot. Whoever was right, her car factory lost money, a tradition that still exists today.

Charles Darwin and the
Origin of Species

Charles Darwin got into terrible trouble because he wrote a book suggesting that people were descended from apes. This annoyed hundreds and hundreds of people, especially those with extra-long hairy arms whose knuckles grazed the ground.

The rediscovery of Australia

Although Australia had been discovered many years before by Captain Cook, in the middle of the nineteenth century the British Government was making a list of all its colonies, and suddenly discovered that Australia was missing. Further investigations revealed that it had been stolen by Professor Moriarty. He had hatched a devilish plot to rule the whole world, and was starting with Australia.

Action was needed, and the Government called in the greatest living detective and money-lender of that time, Shylock Holmes.

'Holmes,' said the Prime Minister, 'the country needs your help. That fiend Professor Moriarty has stolen Australia including all its inhabitants (all seven of them), and Tasmania, and hidden it somewhere. If we do not find it within twenty-four hours, in time for the start of the next Commonwealth Conference, the whole British Empire will collapse.'

'No trouble!' cried Holmes. 'Leave this to me!'

With that Holmes hastened to the scene of the crime, accompanied by his faithful assistant, Dr Whats-On. A close inspection with his magnifying glass revealed what he had already suspected, that where Australia had been there was now just a large area of water. However, with his super eyesight, Holmes spotted a footprint on the surface of the water.

'Quick, Whats-On,' said Holmes. 'Follow that footprint!'

The footprint turned out to be that of a kangaroo that Moriarty had used for his escape after he had stuffed Australia into his suitcase. With two bounds they had followed the kangaroo's footprint to an old wooden shack on the North Island of nearby New Zealand. They hid in a bush just a few metres from the shack, and looked in through the windows. Sure enough, there inside the shack was the villainous Professor Moriarty, hard at work doing his weekly ironing.

'Gad, Holmes!' said the impressed Whats-On. 'How did you deduce that he would be here?'

'Elementary, my dear Smith,' said Holmes (who had a terrible memory for names). 'Kangaroos can only hop across water for a limited length of time before they run out of petrol. This was the nearest place to the scene of the crime, therefore it had to be where the fiendish Professor was making his hide-out.'

'You amaze me, Holmes!' cried Whats-On.

'Sssh!' yelled Holmes. 'He will hear you.'

But Holmes's warning came too late, Whats-On's and Holmes's shouting had alerted Moriarty. He looked up from his ironing, saw the two men in the bush, and at once he acted. First he played the part of King Lear, then he played the parts of Romeo and Juliet, then he grabbed his suitcase (which still contained Australia, Tasmania, and the seven inhabitants), and ran off at great speed.

'After him, Whats-On!' shouted Holmes. 'Call me a taxi!'

'You're a taxi, Holmes,' said Whats-On.

'No, you fool,' said Holmes, 'get us a taxi so that we can chase him.'

But they were out of luck, there were no taxis to be found anywhere in New Zealand.

'What can we do?' groaned Whats-On. 'All is lost. The British Empire will crumble.'

'Not if I can help it,' said Holmes. 'Quick, jump on that ironing board.'

The two men leapt upon Moriarty's ironing board, and slid after him, catching up with the villain just as he reached the coast. With one quick grab, Holmes snatched the suitcase from Moriarty's hand, then he and Whats-On hurtled across the sea on the ironing board, opening the suitcase as they went.

As the suitcase was opened, Australia (and Tasmania, and the seven inhabitants) burst out and landed back where they had originally been, just in time for Holmes and Whats-On to slide up on Bondi Beach on the ironing board. The inhabitants were delighted. Not only had Australia been rediscovered, but surfing had been invented. And that was how Shylock Holmes became the first ever Australian Surfing Champion.

The gold rushes and the San Francisco earthquake

There were three famous gold rushes, two in America and one in Australia. What happened was that someone discovered gold in huge lumps lying about on the ground, and once the word spread everybody wanted to go out and find some. The result was that half the world went off to America and Australia to look for gold. By the time most of them got there, of course, nearly all the gold had already been picked up, so the later arrivals decided to dig for it in case there was some left under the ground.

Most of the gold was actually in California, around the San Francisco area, and soon this area was filled with millions and millions of people, all hard at work digging huge holes, until finally all the digging became too much and the whole city of San Francisco fell down.

Immediately everyone wanted to sue everyone else for the damage to the city, but because there were so many people involved it looked like being an impossible task. After the collapse of San Francisco the police were ordered to arrest everyone with a pick or shovel and lock them up on suspicion of having caused the damage. In just two days they had five million people locked up, each carrying a pick or shovel, and it was costing a fortune to feed them all. Because of this a decision was taken to invent an earthquake and blame the damage on it. This way they could release everyone from the prisons, and no one could sue anybody. This pleased

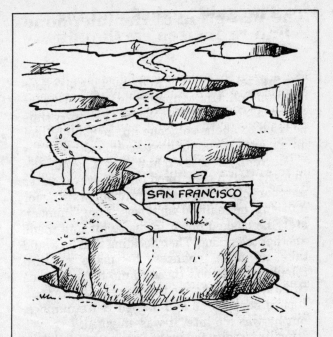

everybody except the lawyers who had hoped
to make millions of dollars out of all the court
cases.

Meanwhile someone had discovered gold in
South Africa, but by this time everyone had got
fed up with the whole business, so they just left
it there until the next generation came along.

The invention of the telephone

The first telephone was invented by Alexander Graham Bell. Unfortunately he forgot to invent a second telephone. This meant that every time he tried to phone someone up, he couldn't get an answer. Also, no one telephoned him.

This really depressed him at first because he thought that no one liked him. However, after ten years of sitting beside his phone waiting for it to ring, he realized what was wrong. Immediately he rushed down to his cellar and made another telephone. Then deciding that he would take no more chances, he made a third telephone. He took these round to his friends Bill and Ben and gave them one each. He then rushed back home and dialled Ben's number, but he was too late, it was engaged.

Feeling really fed up with the whole process by now, he went back down to his cellar and proceeded to invent accessories to his new telephone system to revenge himself on it. These included: the Crossed Line; the Wrong Number; the Number Unobtainable Signal; the Coin Jammed In The Pay Phone Slot; the Constant Funny Noise On The Line; and the Operator Who Won't Listen To You.

Wilbur and Orville Wright

Wilbur and Orville Wright were the first men to fly across the Atlantic Ocean, which they did in 1897. This was a particularly spectacular feat as the aeroplane wasn't invented until 1899.

World War 1

This was the first major war in the entire history of the world. Before then there had always been wars, but they were usually just one country against another. Then the leaders of all the nations of the world had an idea: why not have a World Cup of Wars, in which everyone took part, and the country that was left standing at the end would be the winner.

All the countries thought this was a good idea, because it would mean that all the wars could be fought together in one go instead of dragging on for centuries.

The first problem was choosing a place to hold this competition. No nation wanted it held in their country because of the damage that might

be caused by the supporting fans, but after a vote Europe was selected as the venue.

Kick-off for the first match was 1914 (or nearly a quarter past seven). By 1916 so many millions of people had been either sent off or taken off injured that the organizers began to think that this had not been such a good idea after all. By 1917 (or three minutes after the kick-off) nearly everyone in all the teams was dead, so, with no one left to play, it was decided that the World War was over. In the confusion of everyone dying, no one could really work out who had won. The result of this was more wars that carried on for years as each country fought against everyone else trying to settle the argument as to who had really won. The only result everyone was sure of was that Germany had lost, which annoyed the Germans no end.

Rasputin

Rasputin was a mad monk who was the adviser to the Tsar of Russia on political matters, religious matters, and the price of fresh fish. He was particularly good on the price of tsardines. Apart from that he was a complete and utter nutter and the Tsar's advisers decided that, for the good of Russia, Rasputin had to go. The murder of Rasputin is quite famous in Russia, if not anywhere else, mainly because it took 147 attempts on Rasputin's life before they finally killed him. The first 146 (failed) attempts on Rasputin involved bombs, lasers, man-made earthquakes, machine guns, deadly poisonous snakes, and attempted suffocation in a sea of raspberry jelly. During all this the number of would-be assassins who blew themselves up, lasered themselves, got stung to death, or drowned in the jelly came to a grand total of half a million.

On reflection later historians are of the opinion that this was a high price to pay, even for a man who knew the price of tsardines.

The Russian Revolution

In Russia in 1917 lived a man called Marx. He believed that everyone should be equal, and that there should be no kings or queens or tsars or tsardines. He said that everybody should be brothers. To prove this he got a lot of other people together, told them they were all brothers and then made films about them like *The Marx Brothers Overthrow the Aristocracy*.

Everyone thought this was a good idea, so they held a revolution which overthrew the Russian royal family. Everybody now became brothers. This greatly upset the fifty per cent of the Russian population who were women and said they were sisters. They were so annoyed at Marx for ordering them to be brothers that they decided to overthrow him. They did this by telling everyone that without the tsar there would be no more tsardines. This enraged the Russian people, who loved tinned fish. So there was another revolution in which Marx was overthrown, all his films with his brothers were banned, and the new leaders were Stalin and Leanin (famous as the composer of the song *Leanin on a Lamp-post*).

Picasso

Picasso was a famous artist. He was most
famous for his paintings in which everything
was square or cube-shaped, including the people
who he painted with cubes for heads. Art critics
raved about his 'artistic vision', and collectors
paid millions of pounds for a Picasso painting.
Unfortunately for him and the Art World in
general, his fame collapsed when a journalist
paid him a visit one day, and found that all his
family were in fact square-shaped with block
heads, and that all the animals in the house
were brick-shaped, as was all the food in the
house.

The Wall Street Crash

The Wall Street Crash was a disastrous event in the history of Economy, when all of America thought it had run out of money and the Economy collapsed, leading to The Great Depression, which was the time afterwards when everyone was depressed because no one had any money.

In fact the whole thing was all a mistake and what actually happened was this:

In New York in the 1920s a woman went into a large department store and bought some jewellery. After the clerk had wrapped it up and the time came for her to pay for it, she produced a bag of milk-bottle tops, and when the clerk said, 'That'll be two hundred dollars,' she gave him a small pile of milk-bottle tops as payment. The clerk was worried about this and called for the manager of the store. The manger recognized the woman as the wife of the manager of a large local bank, a business acquaintance, and he was uncertain how to handle the situation. He phoned the bank manager and said, 'Look, I'm sorry to trouble you but this is really embarrassing. Your wife has just come into our store and bought two hundred dollars worth of jewellery, and she has just tried to pay for it with milk-bottle tops.'

'Oh dear,' said the bank manager. 'I'm really terribly sorry about this. You see, she's been under a lot of strain lately. She's been to the doctor, and he suggests that she'll soon snap out of it. If I can ask you to help us, please allow her to use the milk-bottle tops when she comes in to pay for her goods, and then at the end of the month I shall personally come in and pay you what she owes.'

The manager of the department store was very relieved to hear this, and agreed to help the bank manager and his wife, so he told the clerk to accept the milk-bottle tops as payment.

During that month the bank manager's wife came into the store about six times, and each time she paid in milk bottle tops, until in the end she had run up a bill of nearly a thousand dollars. However, as good as his word, at the end of the month the bank manager himself came in, thanked the manager of the department store, and asked how much his wife owed.

'I have the bill here,' said the department store manager. 'The total comes to nine hundred and sixty-five dollars and twelve cents.'

'Fine,' said the bank manager, and he placed a large metal dustbin lid on the counter. 'Do you have change for this dustbin lid?'

It was this one incident that caused the Wall Street crash, because the department store manager believed that the bank had actually run out of money and that the country's whole economy was now based on dustbin lids and milk-bottle tops instead of cash. Of course the truth was that both the bank manager and his wife were completely nuts. However, word spread, and soon the whole of the USA was in chaos as people started giving away their money and trying to buy dustbins and milk-bottle tops instead.

The Irish Question

Lots of people and historians talk about 'The Irish Question', but very few people know what the question actually is. The question is 'Why?' This is because the Irish are an inquisitive people and want to know what is going on, especially in their own country. As a rule no one will tell them.

It all started with the Great Potato Famine in the nineteenth century, when, in order to be able to get hold of a decent bag of crisps, the Irish people had to emigrate to America. This is why most Americans are in fact Irish. (As a note of historical interest, the Irish themselves are descended from Scots, which means that most Irish-Americans are in fact Scottish. This is why, in private, all American presidents are required to wear a kilt at dinner.)

Anyway, here for the first time I am able to reveal the answer to The Irish Question. That answer is: 'Yes.'

The birth of the film industry

Most people think that the film industry started in Hollywood in America. This is not so. It actually started in Sydney, Australia, and all the first silent movies in America (e.g. Charlie Chaplin, Laurel and Hardy) were actually copies of what had happened in Australia just ten years before.

At the beginning of the twentieth century an Australian called Walt Pong had invented a camera that took moving pictures. At first all his friends laughed at him, saying such a thing was impossible. To prove them wrong Walt went out into the bush with his camera determined to come back with some film of real things actually moving.

The first thing he came across was a kangaroo, so he spent a few minutes filming it jumping up and down and backwards and forwards. While he was doing this a group of aborigines appeared, fascinated by Walt's strange behaviour and wanting to see what he was up to. Pleased by having these new subjects appear, Walt pointed the camera at them.

The aborigines were very suspicious at this. In fact they thought that Walt's camera was a new kind of gun and as they were fed up with white Australians coming out into the bush and shooting them they started chucking boomerangs and spears at him. (By doing this they set a tradition of throwing things at people who make films that still carries on today.

People who carry on this tradition are called Film Critics.)

Walt, realizing he was in trouble, immediately set off towards his horse-drawn wagon, dragging his camera with him. He was nearly at his wagon, with the aborigines gaining on him, when suddenly his horse dropped down dead. Walt was stranded, surrounded by angry aborigines! He was doomed!

Suddenly an Australian bushranger appeared, complete with black mask, and ordered the aborigines to put their hands up while he robbed them. (The bushranger wasn't much interested in Walt, who he thought was just a tramp lugging around a big box.) Walt took this opportunity to sneak off to the nearest hiding place so that when the bushranger let the aborigines go they wouldn't know where he was. The nearest building that Walt could see was a wooden outside toilet. He rushed into this, took his clothes off, and then walked out in his long underwear.

Because of his change of appearance the aborigines (now released by the bushranger and feeling pretty annoyed at being robbed) didn't recognize him, and Walt was able to get back to Sydney safely.

Back in Sydney he showed his film to his friends, and found out that not only did he have the bouncing kangaroo on film, he had the rest of his adventures as well, including film of him rushing in and out of the outside toilet and stripping down to his long underwear.

His friends verdict on Walt's film was, 'Rubbish. It'll never catch on.'

Disappointed, Walt threw his camera and his film in a dustbin, where it was found by a visiting American, who watched the film, and stole all Walt's ideas: the bushranger he turned into The Lone Ranger; Walt rushing in and out of the outside toilet he turned into Superman; and the aborigines he turned into Red Indians. As for the kangaroo, he gave it a contract, put a bowler hat and a moustache on it, called it Charlie Chaplin and took it to Hollywood where it made a fortune.

Einstein

Albert Einstein was a very clever man who split the atom, discovered the Theory of Relations, and invented a way to pick your nose without anyone noticing. Because of this last invention he was given the Nobbly Prize for being a Genius.

How he split the atom is easy to explain: he went out and bought a kilo of atoms, then left them in a paper bag by a bus stop so that a bus ran over them.

Much more complex (and therefore harder to explain) is Einstein's Theory of Relations: this says that an aunt in the hand is worth two cousins in a bush. It also uses Pythagoras's Law, which can be explained as follows:

Once there were three brothers in the Sioux tribe in the American Wild West. Their names were Little-Nose, Big-Nose, and No-Nose, and they were in love with three sisters from a neighbouring tribe. These sisters were called Rose Petal, Dandelion, and Dewdrop. The girls' father, He-Who-Sits-On-A-Cactus, agreed that the brothers could marry his daughters, but only if they bought animal skins for his daughters to sit on as marriage presents. Little Nose dutifully turned up with a present of a buffalo skin for Rose Petal, Big Nose bought Dandelion an antelope skin, while No Nose gave Dewdrop the skin of a hippopotamus.

The three couples were then married, and later on each of the three women became preg-

nant. When the children were born Rose Petal had a baby girl, Dandelion had a baby boy, while Dewdrop had twins — one girl and one boy; thus proving Pythagoras's Law that says: the squaw on the hippopotamus hide is equal to the sum of the squaws on the other two hides.

This may not be a lot to do with Albert Einstein and his Theory of Relations, but it's a lot more interesting.

In 1939 an Austrian housepainter of no fixed abode called Adolf Hitler decided that the result of World War Cup I was wrong and called for either a recount or an action replay. After the first World War Cup everyone was a bit dubious as to whether a second was a good idea. However, Hitler insisted, and Germany, who had always been a bit miffed by what they claimed was the unfair result of the first one, supported him.

Once again Europe was picked as the venue for the Big Match. Europe was annoyed at this, claiming it was very unfair. After all, they said, look at the damage the visiting fans had done the first time. So, to appease the Europeans, it was decided to hold some of the qualifying rounds in the Pacific. Europe agreed immediately, but then someone looked at a map and found out that the Pacific was actually a large area of sea and if they sent their troops to march across it they would sink. By this time it was too late as the matches had already got under way, so they had to make do with fighting around bits of the Pacific wherever they could find a patch of ground to stand on.

The result of the Second World War Cup was much the same as the first: nearly everyone died and no one could work out who won. Once again Germany came bottom, this time tying with Italy and Japan.

New countries in the twentieth century

In the middle of the twentieth century there were loads and loads of new countries discovered or invented or that just had their names changed. These included:

1. Israel (1948). Israel was not really a new country. In fact it had been discovered lots of times before by people like Moses and Abraham and the Egyptians and the Romans, but they kept losing it again. Israel became a bit like the ball-point pen of history: every time someone looked round it vanished, and the Israelis had to wait a thousand years or so for it to be found again.

2. Pakistan (1947). Pakistan used to be part of India. Then it became Pakistan. See, that is knowledge.

3. Chile. Chile was not actually a new country in the twentieth century but I wanted to get in the joke about a hot country with a cold name. Chile is a hot country.

The Berlin Wall

As I said before, there are three famous walls in the history of the world. This is the third one.

Many visitors to Berlin have noticed that the Berlin Wall bends and curves rather than going in a straight line. Photographs of the Wall taken from the air show that it is built in the shape of a huge question mark. This is because the Berlin Wall wasn't actually built as a wall at all, and it really is a huge question mark. How it happened was this:

Astronomers in East Germany had for years been trying to make communication with aliens from outer space. Finally a message came through to them on their Space Channel Radio Systems from the far reaches of the Milky Way. It read: 'cmg yfg tht%&n!'

As no one on earth could work out what the message meant, but realizing that it was of vital importance to the planet's future, the astronomers petitioned the East German Government to send back the message: 'What?'

Unfortunately for them the East German Government had decided to cut down its Aliens In Space Research Programme, so they said no. The East German astronomers were really unhappy at this, but then one of them remembered that he had a cousin who was a builder, so the astronomers decided to build their message on the planet's surface, hoping that the aliens would be able to see it from Outer Space with their telescopes.

The next night they started building, working backwards. They had just finished the question mark and were about to start on the giant letter 't', when the Security Forces turned up, arrested the lot of them, and sent them off to build canals in South America. This is why most of the canals that have recently been built in South America seem to be in the shapes of the letters 'Wha'. As soon as they finish the 't' they hope to get an answer.

The Cold War: East versus West

This was a time of great tension. Russia and America were engaged in a Cold War and they brought all their allies into it as well. This meant that Britain and Poland and all the others were involved, and soon half the world was caught up in it.

A Cold War is different from a Hot one because it means you chuck things to do with colds at the other side (germs, tissues, sneezes, etc). America had a major advantage because it had most of the world's handkerchief manufacturers on its side, but Russia had a secret weapon in all the snow it had in Siberia and similar places.

Both sides finally decided to sort it all out with a snowball fight halfway between their two territories, but as this was in the middle of the Atlantic Ocean the snowballs all melted in the water, and the Cold War had to be called off. This was a good thing for the whole world, as the rest of the world was fast running out of tissues, and germs were escaping into countries that weren't even involved in the Cold War.

Stanley Snodgrass

Stanley Snodgrass is a totally uninteresting person but he has paid me to be featured in my *History of the World.* He lives down my street.

The exploration of space

The big achievement of the twentieth century was the discovery of Space. Before, Space had not been discovered at all, it had just been lying there, all endless kilometres of it, with no one taking any notice of it, except the odd astronomer who would look up at it and say things like, 'My heavens, that's a lot of space up there. I must take a look at it some day.'

Then in the middle of the twentieth century came the invention of the rocket. The rocket was created in the Second World War, but after the war stopped the rocket makers looked around for something else to do with their rockets, now they couldn't drop them on people, and that was how Space was discovered.

1. First Man-made Object in Space: This was a telephone booth that was over a gas main that blew up in a High Street in south London. The force of the blast sent the telephone booth out into space, where it proceeded to orbit the earth for the next twelve months. Although it was lucky there was no one in the phone booth at the time of the explosion, if there had been they would have been the First Person in Space, so maybe it wasn't lucky after all, as Science would have advanced many years if that had happened.

2. First Animal in Space: The first animal in space was a caterpillar called Herbert, who went into orbit in 1961. (Although there has been much debate as to whether a caterpillar qualifies as an animal, critics saying that this 'First Animal in Space' title should go to Spot the dog, who went up in 1962. He was lured into a satellite by the cunning means of a bone on a piece of string. Spot went after the bone, and the next thing he knew he was on his way to Jupiter.)

3. First Human in Space: The Russian Cosmonaut, Yuri Flugelhorn. His was a short flight into Space, as the Russians had forgotten to take the elastic band off his rocket, so just as he reached the Outer Atmosphere, the elastic went Twang! and he bounced back to Earth again.

4. First Man on the Moon: This was the American astronaut Neil Down, who fell out of a spaceship that was on its way to Mars. Fortunately for him he had a soft landing on the Moon.

5. First Humans into Outer Space: These were Captain James T Kirk and the crew of the Starship Enterprise. The Enterprise was notable because of its lack of gentlemen's toilets. This meant that the male members of the crew always had to boldly go where no man had gone before. The starship was also unusual in that its First Officer, Mr Spock, had three ears: a left ear, a right ear, and Space, the final front ear.

The Arms Race

The Arms Race was a race between Russia and America to see who could get the most arms. As most arms have a person attached, this meant seeing who could get the most people.

America moved into an early lead by buying up England, Scotland and Wales. This gave them another 68 million people, or 136 million arms.

Russia retaliated by buying up Poland, Czechoslovakia, Hungary and Bulgaria, which had a total of 100 million people. They thought this would give them another 200 million arms, but they hadn't realized that everyone in Bulgaria only had one arm each, thus reducing this total to 137 million arms.

After a few years of this the whole world was in danger of being overrun by arms, so in desperation America and Russia signed a treaty calling for an end to the Arms Race, and switched their competition to legs and feet instead.